The Songs Of Oscar Hammerstein II

SCHIRMER BOOKS
A Division of Macmillan Publishing Co., Inc.
New York

Library of Congress Catalogue Card Number: 74-21637

Published by Williamson Music, Inc. and T.B. Harms Company

Exclusive Music Trade Distributor
Chappell Music Company

PHOTO CREDITS

Blackstone Studios, Inc.: P. 1, 3
Halsman, N.Y.: P. 2
20th Century Fox: P. 145, 217 (bottom), 231, 289 (top right), 307
(top, bottom left)
CBS Television: P. 261
Friedman-Abeles: P. 278 (top left), 289 (top left, bottom)

A special note of thanks is due THE LYNN FARNOL GROUP for its
splendid co-operation in supplying many of the photographs
used in this book.

Another thank you to KEVIN F. MAHONY for invaluable editorial
assistance.

Cover Design: ALAN NAFTAL/STAR

Book Designed and Edited by **LEE SNIDER**

CONTENTS

THE SONGS

OSCAR HAMMERSTEIN II
A GIANT OF THE THEATRE

by LEE SNIDER

Oscar Hammerstein II was a unique and special individual; a highly gifted writer, a superb lyricist, a total man of the theatre, and lastly, a true humanitarian. The heights he scaled in his 65 years of life reflect not only the man's personal successes in his chosen profession, but more deeply, his own heart-felt convictions which he passed on both through his writings and his deeds.

It would serve us well to hear the words of several notable individuals regarding Oscar Hammerstein to gain a further perspective into and appreciation of Hammerstein the man. For he was much more than half of Rodgers &. Moreover, to comprehend his lyrics and contributions to the theatre, one must first know the man himself.

"Oscar Hammerstein was a rare man who wrote rare words and accomplished rare deeds. His legacy includes not only the hundreds of lyric words that are part of our lives but also the burning conviction that there can be a better future for us than the atomization of the world. He believed in a world . . . where justice and peace would rule, and tranquility and good would be an accomplished fact and not an irritating item on the agenda of humankind." — DORE SCHARY

A great cause which Hammerstein espoused was a united world where men could live together in peace and harmony. Toward this end he gave of himself tirelessly as a member of the United World Federalists. His was a dream for peace, brotherhood, and a community of nations governed by law. The lyric he wrote for "Happy Talk" in SOUTH PACIFIC expresses Oscar's viewpoint most succinctly:

"If you don' have a dream,
How you gonna have a dream come true?"

Hammerstein was a man of many dreams!

"As Oscar so clearly understood, our planet is too small and too dangerous to be governed by anything but law. That was Oscar's aim . . ." — ADLAI E. STEVENSON

"Oscar Hammerstein's vision was not limited by the boundless, yet confined, arena of the theatre. He was . . . deeply sensitive equally to human emotion and to human folly. Hatred was his chief abomination." — THE RT. HON. EARL ATLEE

Remember the lyric from SOUTH PACIFIC in which Lt. Cable sings —

"You've got to be taught before it's too late,
Before you are six or seven or eight,
To hate all the people your relatives hate,
You've got to be carefully taught!"

On a professional level, Richard Rodgers surely knew Oscar Hammerstein better than most. Their succession of brilliant musical plays from OKLAHOMA! in 1943 to their last show THE SOUND OF MUSIC in 1959 revolutionized the musical theatre. As Rodgers commented in 1959: " . . . he [Hammerstein] is a curious study in contrasts . . . he is extraordinarily gentle and yet I've seen

Oscar Hammerstein II during his years at Columbia University

him rise to horrendous heights of fury. These furies, however, are almost always directed in one way against injustice. He is a passionately loving man and yet any overt expression of this love I've never seen anywhere except in his work. He's a meticulously hard worker and yet he'll roam the grass of his farm for hours and sometimes even days before he can bring himself to put a word on paper. In the past few years it's become chic . . .

to regard 'love' as somewhat of a dirty word. Oscar has always been an exponent of quite the opposite theory . . ."

An early photo of Oscar Hammerstein with his wife Dorothy.

In November of 1961 Winthrop Sargeant, writing in THE NEW YORKER MAGAZINE, concisely summed up Oscar Hammerstein II: "an unabashed sentimentalist, a believer in optimism, religion, noble causes, and wholesome living." He was ". . . a large man of affectionate disposition . . . a much respected figure in the theatrical and literary worlds . . ." who ". . . had little or no gift for satire. He lacked the bitterness of the true satirist,

and he found real life a wonderful thing. But he was a very skillful lyric-writer . . . It was inevitable that he should give the . . . musical show a new atmosphere — one in which the accent was on romantic love, political idealism, tolerance, and serious . . . dramatic ideas."

Yes, he favoured simple, romantic love:

"I'm as corny as Kansas in August,
I'm as normal as blueberry pie.
No more a smart
Little girl with no heart,
I have found me a wonderful guy."
— SOUTH PACIFIC

And true romantic eloquence:

"I hear music when I look at you
A beautiful theme of ev'ry dream I ever knew
Down deep in my heart
I hear it play,
I feel it start,
Then melt away.
I hear music when I touch your hand,
A beautiful melody from some enchanted land,
Down deep in my heart,
I hear it say,
Is this the day?"
— MUSIC IN THE AIR

And his words expressed optimism:

"A hundred million miracles
Are happening every day.
And those who say they don't agree,
Are those who do not hear or see."
— FLOWER DRUM SONG

He could poignantly express the feelings of the common man:

"You an' me, we sweat an' strain
Body all achin' an' racked wid pain
Tote dat barge!
Lift dat bale!
Git a little drunk
An' you land in jail."
— SHOW BOAT

At times even sophistication à la Cole Porter:

"All in fun,
This thing is all in fun,
When all is said and done
How far can it go?
Some cocktails;
Some orchids,
A show or two,
A line in a column
That links me with you."
— VERY WARM FOR MAY

The economy of words with which Hammerstein could meaningfully express emotion through the sheer usage of poetry is reflected in this totally uplifting lyric:

"When you walk through a storm
Keep your chin up high
And don't be afraid of the dark.
At the end of the storm
Is a golden sky
And the sweet silver song
Of the lark.
Walk on
Through the wind
Walk on through the rain
Though your dreams be tossed and blown.

Walk on
Walk on
With hope in your heart
And you'll never walk alone."
— CAROUSEL

Oscar Hammerstein II was born on July 12, 1895 in New York City, the grandson of Oscar Hammerstein I, a grand opera impresario who spent most of his fortune building theatres and trying to make opera pay. His father, William Hammerstein, was a theatre manager and for many years director of Hammerstein's Victoria, the most popular vaudeville theatre of its day.

Hammerstein went to Columbia University and studied law where his main theatrical connection was writing the book and lyrics for Columbia's Varsity Show entitled HOME, JAMES. At a performance of this show Hammerstein was introduced to the very young Richard Rodgers who had seen the show with his older brother, then a Sophomore at Columbia. Though this meeting was in 1917, it was not until 1943 that the two men teamed to become theatrical legends.

Working in a law office did not suit Oscar Hammerstein and after one year he felt certain his future lay in the theatre and not in the law courts. Taking a job with his uncle, Arthur Hammerstein, he became an assistant stage manager for $20 per week. And this despite some sound advice from his father: "Don't ever smoke cigars!" and "Stay out of the theatre!" In 1919 he was promoted to general stage manager. His first play in this capacity was called SOMETIME and starred Ed Wynn and Mae West. The sultry Miss West had some advice for young Oscar, too: "Go back to law, kid. The theatre ain't for you. You got too much class!"

Undaunted, Hammerstein wrote a play called THE LIGHT — it went dark in less than a week. Next came TICKLE ME for comedian Frank Tinney. Opening night Tinney closed Act II by announcing to the audience: "The rest of this play is a gimmick that won't work. I tell you now the guy gets the girl so you can go home and get some sleep."

In 1922 he scored his first success as a librettist when he co-authored WILDFLOWER with Otto Harbach. The music was by Vincent Youmans, and the play ran 15 months. Encouraged, he then wrote four successive flops. The critic known for his acid wit, Alexander Woolcott, wrote of one: "Oscar Hammerstein and Milton Gropper . . . wrote a comedy that came a cropper."

1924, however, reversed the tide when he teamed with Harbach and Rudolf Friml. The happy result was the classic operetta ROSE-MARIE. The following year came SUNNY, set to the music of Jerome Kern, then THE DESERT SONG in 1926 with Sigmund Romberg providing the memorable music. His next venture was entitled GOLDEN DAWN, notable only for the presence of a young Englishman named Archie Leach. Mr. Leach was later to achieve fame as Cary Grant.

1927 marked a turning point in Hammerstein's career. He and Kern wrote SHOW BOAT, likely the most important musical play of its time. Based on Edna Ferber's best-selling novel, SHOW BOAT was a dramatic step forward in the evolution of the musical play in that the songs, dances and story were formed into an integrated whole. SHOW BOAT enjoyed a lengthy run at the Ziegfeld Theatre while Hammerstein went on to write THE NEW MOON (music by Romberg), GOOD BOY, and SWEET ADELINE (music by Kern) in which the great blues singer

Helen Morgan introduced "Why Was I Born?" Though a hit, SWEET ADELINE was done in by the stock market crash of 1929.

Hollywood beckoned and Hammerstein went west to do four films for Warner Bros. Apparently unhappy with the results of the first two, Warner's paid him $100,000 <u>not</u> to make the last two. The theatre, however, was Hammerstein's true calling and in 1932 he wrote MUSIC IN THE AIR to Jerome Kern's enchanting score; in 1935 came MAY WINE with Sigmund Romberg, and in 1939 VERY WARM FOR MAY, Kern's last Broadway show. Though the latter was a dismal flop, it contained one of their most beautiful songs, "All The Things You Are." SUNNY RIVER, written with Romberg in 1941, was another bomb, and Hammerstein retired to his Doylestown, Pennsylvania farm in despair. Up until this time his career had seen a number of great successes, but many dismal failures dogged his steps. Perhaps Mae West's words many years before had been wiser than he'd thought.

Idly seeking something new with which to occupy himself, Hammerstein commenced writing a modern version of Bizet's opera CARMEN in 1942. A telephone call from Richard Rodgers caused the lyricist to put his project aside, though only temporarily. Rodgers had a play called GREEN GROW THE LILACS by Lynn Riggs which he felt would make a good musical. His partner, Lorenz Hart, wished no part of it. Would Hammerstein be interested?

Oscar Hammerstein II as a child, and in the mid-1930's at MGM.

Rodgers and Hammerstein at work on the score for SOUTH PACIFIC, 1949.

The result was AWAY WE GO, which became OKLAHOMA! and the rest is history. Not all was smooth going. The title interested no one. A cast principal even suggested they discard a song called "People Will Say We're In Love." With little fanfare, bad word of mouth from out of town, and an opening night audience only two-thirds full, OKLAHOMA! bowed on March 31, 1943 at the St. James Theatre. As Alfred Drake appeared on stage singing "Oh, What A Beautiful Mornin'" an audible gasp permeated the theatre — the magic had begun and it continued right through to the play's conclusion.

The utter simplicity of the song which so perfectly set the mood for OKLAHOMA! was inspired, as Oscar later confided, when ". . . I remembered an actual morning on a Pennsylvania farm." It was Hammerstein's contention that the great secret of a well-integrated musical play is the wielding of words and melodies into a single expression. Moreover, lyrics have to be phonetically singable. The original lyric to "Oh, What A Beautiful Mornin'" had the "corn as high as a cowpony's eye." Although perfectly suitable as to meaning and rhythm, cowpony was rejected as being too difficult to sing. Hence the substituted word elephant!

OKLAHOMA! commenced a second productive phase of Hammerstein's career and simultaneously launched a partnership that has remained unparalleled in the history of the theatre. It was Hammerstein's opinion that the secret of his successful collaboration with Rodgers lay in their amazing affinity and similar backgrounds. "Our social lives, our personal habits, are similar, our theatrical tastes and standards are identical." Elaborating further, he noted that "sometimes, I write the lyrics first and Rodgers sets them to music. Sometimes he has a wonderful idea for a scene and writes the music first. I have only one complaint. It takes me weeks to write a song lyric. Dick often turns out the melody in an hour." Rodgers concurs, noting that ". . . I don't believe that it can be said that we're a couple of idiots living in a blissful state of euphoria, and it's perfectly true that we can and do disagree over an idea, a rhyme or certain technical usages. But I've always felt the fact that we get on so well together is due essentially to the circumstance that our basic philosophies are so much alike."

Hammerstein then returned to CARMEN. Retitled CARMEN JONES and produced by Billy Rose, it became a modern retelling of the Prosper Merimée story with a Black cast. Some years later it became a successful film with the late Dorothy Dandridge in the title role.

In 1945 R & H converted Ferenc Molnar's LILIOM into CAROUSEL. Taken out of its Hungarian locale and transferred to the Maine seacoast, CAROUSEL was a tremendous success and boasts one of the finest scores ever written by Rodgers & Hammerstein. Then came the film musical STATE FAIR which won an Oscar for its song "It Might As Well Be Spring."

Not content simply writing for the theatre, R & H expanded their activities by producing John van Druten's comedy I REMEMBER MAMA and in May of 1946 produced Irving Berlin's greatest hit, ANNIE GET YOUR GUN starring the inimitable Ethel Merman. Continuing the trend of a new stage musical every other year, the team's next project was an original musical. The result was ALLEGRO, a charming and beguiling musical with a contemporary and completely American setting. Furthermore, it was Hammerstein's first original book of the young partnership and to both men it meant a great deal personally. Writing in OPERA NEWS, Feb. 25, 1961 Rodgers says Hammerstein "... admitted that in ALLEGRO he came the closest he had ever come to autobiography. The main character was a doctor. ALLEGRO was not, however, a medical musical, but rather a modern morality play exploring the problem of personal integrity in today's fast-moving, success-oriented society..

Despite an advance sale of a half million dollars, ALLEGRO failed to achieve hit status. Even with its highly original, inventive score, resourceful book, and creative staging by Agnes de Mille, the play did not catch on and closed after a disappointing run of 315 performances.

The year was 1949. The play was SOUTH PACIFIC, fashioned from James A. Michener's Pulitzer-Prize winning novel "Tales of the South Pacific." The critical verdict — a Rodgers & Hammerstein masterpiece. Mary Martin as Ensign Nellie Forbush and Ezio Pinza of the Metropolitan Opera in the role of Emile DeBecque proved inspired casting. To have heard Pinza sing "Some Enchanted Evening" is to have experienced the ultimate drama and emotional impact to be found in the most inspired form of writing for the musical stage. Hammerstein commenting on building his word pictures to music: "When I wrote 'I'm in love with a wonderful guy' I had in mind a glimpse of Mary Martin in a gingham dress six years before."

There were occasions when Hammerstein's thea-

trical expertise added to Rodgers' music. "Oscar had written the lyric ["A Wonderful Guy"] and turned it over to me," says Rodgers, "with the simple finish 'I'm in love with a wonderful guy.' When I played him the music I had written for his words, he jumped out of his chair and said, 'Why don't you repeat I'm in love, I'm in love, I'm in love as often as you think you can with increasing intensity? It might give the feeling of exultation and express the girl's great joy over her love for this man.' The result in the theatre was that Mary Martin reached a peak of near-hysteria at the end of the song and brought down the house at every performance. This lyric is a perfect example of Oscar's phenomenal talent for construction."

Mr. & Mrs. Rodgers, Mr. & Mrs. Hammerstein II — the opening of the film version of THE KING AND I.

Proceeding geographically from the South Pacific islands, R & H moved on to the Orient for their next musical play. Based on Margaret Landon's book "Anna And The King Of Siam," their version was entitled THE KING AND I. Though topping SOUTH PACIFIC seemed nothing short of a Herculean task, THE KING AND I was a sensation and proved a most worthy successor. With the great Gertrude Lawrence and a magnetic Yul Brynner in the leads, THE KING AND I enjoyed a long-running tenancy at the St. James Theatre. Sadly, it was to be Gertrude Lawrence's last role — she died during the run of the play.

ME AND JULIET, Rodgers and Hammerstein's valentine to their profession, the theatre, bowed in 1953. Of interest is "No Other Love" which came from the superb symphonic score Rodgers had written for the NBC-TV presentation of VICTORY AT SEA. Feeling that the melody from the segment entitled "Beneath The Southern

Oscar Hammerstein receiving an honorary Doctorate of Humane Letters from Boston University President Harold C. Case, June, 1957.

Cross" could stand on its own as a popular song, Rodgers had Hammerstein set lyrics to it. The result was the lovely ballad "No Other Love."

In 1955 the team wrote PIPE DREAM based on John Steinbeck's Cannery Row classic "Sweet Thursday" in which opera singer Helen Traubel made her Broadway debut. Their only joint venture for television was the 1957 spectacular CINDERELLA with Julie Andrews in the title role. CBS-TV later mounted a new version featuring Leslie Ann Warren as Cinderella that has since become an annual TV treat. The clashing of ancient traditions and modern-day youth in San Francisco's Chinatown provided the background for the 1958 musical FLOWER DRUM SONG based on the novel by C.Y. Lee. Starring Miyoshi Umeki and Pat Suzuki along with veterans Keye Luke and Juanita Hall (the original Bloody Mary in SOUTH PACIFIC), FLOWER DRUM SONG was a visual and aural delight playing on Broadway for 600 performances.

The last show to bear the trademark Music by Richard Rodgers/Lyrics by Oscar Hammerstein II was THE SOUND OF MUSIC which opened November 16, 1959 at the Lunt-Fontanne Theatre. Howard Lindsay and Russell Crouse, the authors of LIFE WITH FATHER, provided the book and Mary Martin gave one of her finest performances as Maria von Trapp. Despite the mixed reviews from the critics, Rodgers later said, ". . . it is curious that the play running in New York this season to the greatest number of people and to the largest amount of money, THE SOUND OF MUSIC, is concerned with a young Catholic girl about to become a nun and her friends. Somebody down here likes us."

In addition to his collaboration with Rodgers, Oscar Hammerstein found the time to write scenarios and lyrics for several major motion pictures including SHOW BOAT, SWING HIGH SWING LOW, HIGH WIDE AND HANDSOME, and THE STORY OF VERNON AND IRENE CASTLE. He also wrote the lyrics for the screen version of THE GREAT WALTZ. In 1955 Rodgers & Hammerstein

Rodgers & Hammerstein writing "Don't Marry Me" in Boston during a rehearsal of FLOWER DRUM SONG (1958).

Hammerstein at the 1956 Chicagoland Festival.

Admiring "Immutable Images" Award in Oklahoma City, Feb. 1960.

produced the Todd-AO film version of OKLAHOMA! and in 1958 the movie of SOUTH PACIFIC. Other R & H musicals made into popular films were CAROUSEL, THE KING AND I, FLOWER DRUM SONG and THE SOUND OF MUSIC which became one of the most successful and highest-grossing movies of all time.

While virtually all of Hammerstein's song lyrics were written for musical plays or films, several notable exceptions bear mention. "The Last Time I Saw Paris" was written in 1940 with Jerome Kern; another Kern opus to which Hammerstein wrote lyrics was "The Sweetest Sight I Have Seen." With Rodgers he wrote several songs during World War II — "Steady As You Go — The P.T. Boat Song" and a song for the Infantry — "We're On Our Way."

Rodgers and Hammerstein, separately and together, have been the recipients of innumerable awards. To mention but a few: a Special Award from the Pulitzer Prize Committee for OKLAHOMA! and a Special Citation by the N.Y. Critics' Circle for CAROUSEL; to Hammerstein, the Donaldson Award for the book and lyrics of CARMEN JONES, CAROUSEL, ALLEGRO, and SOUTH PACIFIC; the

Oscar for "The Last Time I Saw Paris"; for SOUTH PACIFIC, the Pulitzer Prize for Drama, the N.Y. Critics' Circle for Best Musical, and the Tony Award for his part in producing and writing the musical.

On August 23, 1960 Oscar Hammerstein II died at his farm in Doylestown, Pennsylvania. He was 65 years old. His songs have become an integral part of our national heritage as have his many musical plays. Their context, as expressed through Hammerstein's superb mastery of his craft in wielding words of drama and poetry to connote ideals and emotions, is nothing short of universal. His is a rich and bountiful legacy and by his contributions and deeds he has earned for himself a place among the highest echelons of writers for the theatre. The precedents he established both in the structural growth of the form known as musical theatre and the lyrics he wrote will continue to guide all who write for theatre as they, in their own ways, attempt to further add to the continually evolving musical play. That his presence will always be felt can be found in a song title Oscar Hammerstein wrote for ALLEGRO — "You Are Never Away."

ROSE-MARIE

Lyrics by **OTTO HARBACH & OSCAR HAMMERSTEIN II** / Music by **RUDOLF FRIML**   **ROSE-MARIE** (1924)

INDIAN LOVE CALL

Lyrics by **OTTO HARBACH & OSCAR HAMMERSTEIN II** / Music by **RUDOLF FRIML**   ROSE-MARIE (1924)

17

If you re-fuse me, I will be blue____ And wait-ing all a-lone; But if when you hear____ my love call____ ring-ing clear, And I hear your an - swer-ing ech - o, so dear,____ Then I will know_____ our love will come true,____ You'll be-long to me,____ I'll be-long to you!

WHO?

Lyrics by **OTTO HARBACH & OSCAR HAMMERSTEIN II** / Music by **JEROME KERN**

means my hap - pi - ness, Who
would I an - swer: yes, to?
Well, you ought — to guess who,
—Darned if I — can guess who,
no one but you.
no one but you.

THE RIFF SONG

Lyrics by **OTTO HARBACH & OSCAR HAMMERSTEIN II** / Music by **SIGMUND ROMBERG**

THE DESERT SONG (1926)

The classic operetta, ROSE-MARIE, was made into a film in 1936. Seen above are James Stewart and Jeanette MacDonald with Nelson Eddy as a dashing Canadian Mountie.

Left: Ray Bolger and English musical star Anna Neagle appeared in the movie version of SUNNY (1941). Above: The original cast of SUNNY with (from left to right) Joseph Cawthorn, Dorothy Francis, Clifton Webb, Marilyn Miller, Paul Frawley, Mary Hay, and Jack Donahue.

ONE ALONE

Lyrics by **OTTO HARBACH & OSCAR HAMMERSTEIN II** / Music by **SIGMUND ROMBERG**

THE DESERT SONG (1926)

All the world for-got-ten In one wo-man's smile.

REFRAIN
(Andante moderato)

One a - lone _____ to be my own,

I a - lone _____ to know her ca - ress - es;

One to be _____ e - ter - nal - ly _____ The

Irene Manning, Bruce Cabot, and Dennis Morgan in Hollywood's 1943 treatment of THE DESERT SONG.

Left: William O'Neal, Margaret Irving, and Lyle Evans in the original production of THE DESERT SONG. Center: SHOW BOAT - the original cast includes Allan Campbell, Charles Ellis, Helen Morgan, Eva Puck, Norma Terris (kneeling), Charles Winninger, and Edna May Oliver. Right: Original sheet music title page for SUNNY.

Left: Norma Terris as Magnolia, Charles Winninger as Captain Andy in SHOW BOAT. Center: Buddy Ebsen, Colette Lyons, Ralph Dumke, Carol Bruce, and Robert Allen in the 1946 revival of SHOW BOAT. Right: Helen Morgan, the original Julie.

THE DESERT SONG

Lyrics by **OTTO HARBACH & OSCAR HAMMERSTEIN II** / Music by **SIGMUND ROMBERG**

THE DESERT SONG (1926)

CAN'T HELP LOVIN' DAT MAN

Lyrics by **OSCAR HAMMERSTEIN** II / Music by **JEROME KERN**

SHOW BOAT (1927)

tell me he's slow,— Tell me I'm cra - zy, may-be, I know,—

Can't help lov - in' dat man— of mine.——

cresc. e piu appass.

When he goes a - way

Dat's a rain - y day, And when he comes

Above: Charles Winninger and the "SHOW BOAT audience" (1927). Below left: Constance Towers as Julie and William Traylor in the 1966 Lincoln Center revival. Below right: Norma Terris and Howard Marsh in the original production.

MAKE BELIEVE

Lyrics by **OSCAR HAMMERSTEIN** II / Music by **JEROME KERN**

SHOW BOAT (1927)

And if the things we dream a - bout don't hap - pen_ to be so, ____

That's just an un - im - por - tant tech - ni - cal - i - ty. ____

REFRAIN

At a slow even pace (expressively)

We could make be - lieve ____ I love you, ____ On - ly make be - lieve ____

that you love me. ____ Oth - ers find peace of mind in pre -

YOU ARE LOVE

Lyrics by **OSCAR HAMMERSTEIN** II / Music by **JEROME KERN**

Once a wan-d'ring ne'er-do - well, Just a va-grant rov-ing fel-low, I went my way. —— Life was just a joke to tell, Like a lone-ly Pun - chi - nel - lo My role

You ——————— are love, ——

Won-der of all the world.—— Where you go with

me Heav-en will al - ways be!——

me Heav-en will al - ways be!——

WHY DO I LOVE YOU ?

Lyrics by **OSCAR HAMMERSTEIN** II / Music by **JEROME KERN**

SHOW BOAT (1927)

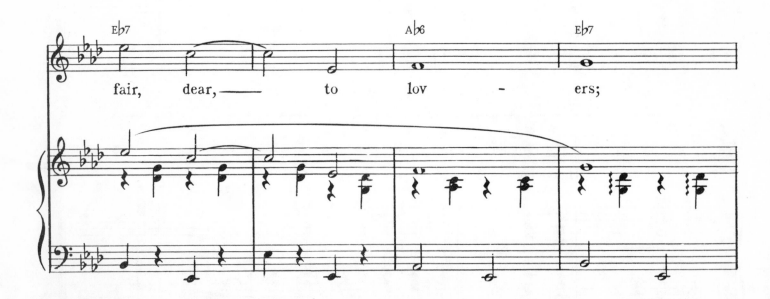

Above: Buddy Ebsen and Colette Lyons in the show-stopping "Goodbye My Lady Love" from the 1946 SHOW BOAT revival. Below: Original and 1946 revival sheet music title pages. Center: The company from the original 1927 production of SHOW BOAT.

OL' MAN RIVER

Lyrics by **OSCAR HAMMERSTEIN** II / Music by **JEROME KERN**

SHOW BOAT (1927)

STOUTHEARTED MEN

Lyrics by **OSCAR HAMMERSTEIN II** / Music by **SIGMUND ROMBERG**

THE NEW MOON (1928)

LOVER, COME BACK TO ME!

Lyrics by **OSCAR HAMMERSTEIN II** / Music by **SIGMUND ROMBERG**

THE NEW MOON (1928)

met you   Seems to stay for-ev-er in my mind.

REFRAIN

The sky was blue,   And high a-bove   The moon was new

And so was love.   This eag-er heart of mine was sing - ing:

"Lov- er, where can you be?"_____   You came at last,

walked a - long with you, No won - der I am lone - ly.

The sky is blue, The night is cold, The moon is new,

But love is old, And, while I'm wait-ing here, This heart of mine is sing-ing:

"Lov - er come back to me!" me!"

WANTING YOU

Lyrics by **OSCAR HAMMERSTEIN** II / Music by **SIGMUND ROMBERG**

THE **NEW MOON** (1928)

My heart is ach-ing for some - one, And you are that some - one;

You know the truth of my sto - ry, You must be-lieve what you see.___

I too, may some day love some - one, From some -
where, there'll come one; One who will hear the same sto -
ry That you're tell-ing me.

REFRAIN Andante espressivo

Want-ing you,___ ev-'ry day I am want-ing you,___ Ev-'ry night I am

71

long - ing to _____ Hold you close to my ea - ger breast;

Want-ing love, _____ in that heav-en I'm dream-ing of _____ Makes that heav - en seem

far a - bove _____ An - y hope that I'll gain my quest. _____

Molto espressivo

Dreams are vain, _____ But I cling to the mer - est

agitato

chance that you may hear me: Dreams are vain,_____ For when-

ever I wake I nev-er find you near me.

Wanting you,___ nothing else in this world will do,___ In this world you are

all that I a-dore._____ All I a-dore.

DON'T EVER LEAVE ME

IRENE DUNNE

'SWEET ADELINE'

JEROME KERN

OSCAR HAMMERSTEIN II

$1.00

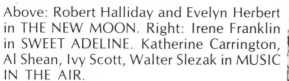

Above: Robert Halliday and Evelyn Herbert in THE NEW MOON. Right: Irene Franklin in SWEET ADELINE. Katherine Carrington, Al Shean, Ivy Scott, Walter Slezak in MUSIC IN THE AIR.

Above: SWEET ADELINE - sheet music cover featuring Irene Dunne in the Warner Bros. film. Below: A scene from the SWEET ADELINE movie version as carriages leave Hammersteins Theatre after attending "The Love Song" as displayed under the marquee.

DON'T EVER LEAVE ME

Lyrics by **OSCAR HAMMERSTEIN** II / Music by **JEROME KERN**

SWEET ADELINE (1929)

WHY WAS I BORN?

Lyrics by **OSCAR HAMMERSTEIN** II / Music by **JEROME KERN**

SWEET ADELINE (1929)

I'VE TOLD EV'RY LITTLE STAR

Lyrics by **OSCAR HAMMERSTEIN** II / Music by **JEROME KERN**

THE SONG IS YOU

Lyrics by **OSCAR HAMMERSTEIN** II / Music by **JEROME KERN**

MUSIC IN THE AIR (1932)

let you know the song my heart would sing,_____ That beau-ti-ful

rhap-so-dy of love and youth and spring_____ The mu-sic is

sweet,_____ The words are true,_____ The song is

you._____

A tranquil scene from MUSIC IN THE AIR shows Katherine Carrington, Reinald Werrenrath (standing) and Walter Slezak. Below: Original sheet music title pages for MUSIC IN THE AIR, HIGH WIDE AND HANDSOME (film) and VERY WARM FOR MAY (Jerome Kern's last Broadway musical).

THE FOLKS WHO LIVE ON THE HILL

Lyrics by **OSCAR HAMMERSTEIN** II / Music by **JEROME KERN**   *HIGH, WIDE AND HANDSOME* (1937)

ALL THE THINGS YOU ARE

Lyrics by **OSCAR HAMMERSTEIN II** / Music by **JEROME KERN**

VERY WARM FOR MAY (1939)

Touch - ing your hand, my heart beats the fast - er, All that I want in all of this world is you.

REFRAIN

You are the prom - ised kiss of spring - time That makes the lone - ly win - ter seem long.

Some day my hap-py arms will hold you, And some day I'll know that mo-ment di-vine, When all the things you are, are mine!

mine!

ALL IN FUN

Lyrics by **OSCAR HAMMERSTEIN** II / Music by **JEROME KERN**

VERY WARM FOR MAY (1939)

Oscar Hammerstein II with two notable collaborators during the 1920's and 1930's. Above: Jerome Kern at the piano with whom Hammerstein wrote such enduring classics as SHOW BOAT, SUNNY, MUSIC IN THE AIR, and CENTENNIAL SUMMER. At left: Sigmund Romberg, Oscar Hammerstein, and Jerome Kern at the Hammerstein home in Hollywood. Even today Romberg and Hammerstein's great operettas THE DESERT SONG and THE NEW MOON remain popular favourites.

THE THEATRE GUILD

presents

Oklahoma!

A Musical Play Based on the play
"GREEN GROW THE LILACS" by LYNN RIGGS

Music by
RICHARD RODGERS
Book and Lyrics by
OSCAR HAMMERSTEIN 2d
Production directed by
ROUBEN MAMOULIAN
Dances by
AGNES de MILLE

Settings by LEMUEL AYERS · Costumes by MILES WHITE

With

BETTY GARDE · ALFRED DRAKE · JOSEPH BULOFF
JOAN ROBERTS · LEE DIXON · HOWARD da SILVA
CELESTE HOLM · RALPH RIGGS · MARC PLATT
GEORGE CHURCH · KATHARINE SERGAVA
Orchestra directed by JACOB SCHWARTZDORF
Orchestrations by RUSSELL BENNETT

Production under the supervision of
THERESA HELBURN & LAWRENCE LANGNER

A page from the OKLAHOMA! Souvenir Program during its 2, 248 performance run.

105

IN THE HEART OF THE DARK

Lyrics by **OSCAR HAMMERSTEIN** II / Music by **JEROME KERN**

VERY WARM FOR MAY (1939)

And soon you ar - rive, _____ The moon in your hair, _____ The night is a - live While _ you are there, _____ In _____ the heart of the dark. _____ I know the sun's on its way _

OKLAHOMA

Lyrics by **OSCAR HAMMERSTEIN** II / Music by **RICHARD RODGERS**

OKLAHOMA! (1943)

plen'-y of room, Plen'-y of room to swing a rope! ____

Plen'-y of heart and plen'-y of hope. ___

REFRAIN
(Lustily)

O _____ k - la-hom-a, where the wind comes sweep-in' down the

plain _____ And the wav - in' wheat can sure smell sweet When the

I CAIN'T SAY NO

Lyrics by **OSCAR HAMMERSTEIN** II / Music by **RICHARD RODGERS**

OKLAHOMA! (1943)

OKLAHOMA! made history opening night March 31, 1943, with its unique blending of songs, story and dance. Above: The company. Below right: BETTY GARDE, JOAN ROBERTS and ALFRED DRAKE. Below left: KATHERINE SERGAVA in AGNES DeMILLE'S famous Dream Ballet — "Laurey Makes Up Her Mind."

MANY A NEW DAY

Lyrics by **OSCAR HAMMERSTEIN** II / Music by **RICHARD RODGERS**

OKLAHOMA! (1943)

man I lose is the on-ly man a-mong men. I'll snap my fin-gers to show I don't care; I'll buy me a brand new dress to wear; I'll scrub my neck and I'll brush my hair, And start in o-ver a-gain

REFRAIN

Man-y a new face will please my eye, Man-y a new love will find me;

Nev-er-'ve I wan-dered through the rye, won-der-ing where has some guy gone;

1. Man - y a new day will dawn be-fore I do!

2. dawn ___ Man - y a red sun will set! Man - y a blue moon will

shine be-fore I do! ___

OH, WHAT A BEAUTIFUL MORNIN'

Lyrics by **OSCAR HAMMERSTEIN II** / Music by **RICHARD RODGERS**

OKLAHOMA! (1943)

Above: Oscar Hammerstein II and Richard Rodgers cut cake at birthday party for OKLAHOMA! and CAROUSEL. (Photo by Cosmo-Sileo). Below: The company, featuring John Raitt (on podium at left) as Billy Bigelow in CAROUSEL. Other illustrations are sheet music covers for OKLAHOMA!, CARMEN JONES (film version), and CAROUSEL, plus Playbill cover for OKLAHOMA!

PORE JUD

Lyrics by **OSCAR HAMMERSTEIN** II / Music by **RICHARD RODGERS**

OKLAHOMA! (1943)

folks 'at real-ly knowed him,

G7 *(Chanting)*

knowed 'at beneath them two dirty shirts he always wore, there

C7

beat a heart as big as all out - doors.

F

JUD: C7

As big as all out -

F CURLY: C7

doors. Jud Fry loved his fel-low man.

F JUD: C7

He loved his fel-low man.

F

G#m7   C#7   F#m   F#m6   G#m   B7

CURLY: *(speaks)*

He loved the birds of the forest and the beasts of the field. He loved the mice and the vermin in the barn, and he treated the rats like equals, which was right.

And he loved little children. He loved ev'body and ev'thin' in the world! On'y he never let on, so nobody ever knowed it!

CURLY:

Pore Jud is daid. Pore Jud Fry is daid! His friends-'ll weep and wail for miles a-

JUD: (Miles a-round.)   CURLY:

round. _____ The dais - ies in the dell Will give

out a diff-'rent smell, Be - cuz por Jud is un - der - neath the ground.

DAT'S LOVE

Lyrics by **OSCAR HAMMERSTEIN** II / Music by **GEORGES BIZET**
Adapted by Robert Russell Bennett

CARMEN JONES (1943)

135

CAROUSEL, boasting one of Rodgers and Hammerstein's most beautiful scores, was made into a delightful film in 1956, eleven years after its Broadway opening.

20th Century-Fox
presents

RODGERS and HAMMERSTEIN'S

CAROUSEL

CinemaScope
55
THE NEW DIMENSION IN SIGHT AND SOUND

starring GORDON MAC RAE
SHIRLEY JONES
with CAMERON MITCHELL
Produced by HENRY EPHRON
Directed by HENRY KING
Screenplay by PHOEBE and HENRY EPHRON
From the Stage Play "Liliom" by Ferenc Molnar
and the Musical Stage Hit by Rodgers & Hammerstein

BEAT OUT THAT RHYTHM ON A DRUM

Lyrics by **OSCAR HAMMERSTEIN** II / Music by **GEORGES BIZET**
Adapted by Robert Russell Bennett

CARMEN JONES (1943)

140

142

144

Barbara Ruick as Carrie Pipperidge and Robert Rounsville as Capt. Enoch Snow in the film of CAROUSEL. Bottom: Rod Alexander's spirited dances gave great zest to "June Is Bustin' Out All Over."

IF I LOVED YOU

Lyrics by **OSCAR HAMMERSTEIN** II / Music by **RICHARD RODGERS**

CAROUSEL (1945)

Allegretto moderato

When I worked in the mill, Weav-in' at the loom, I'd gaze ab-sent-
Kind-a scraw-ny and pale, Pick-in' at my food And love-sick like

mind-ed at the roof _____ And half the time the shut-tle 'd
an-y oth-er guy _____ I'd throw a-way my sweat-er and

tan-gle in the threads, And the warp 'd get mixed with the woof _____
dress up like a dude In a dick-ey and a col-lar and a tie _____

by! Soon you'd leave me, off — you would go — in the

mist of day, Nev - er, nev - er to know _____

_____ How I loved you, If I

loved you. _____ loved you. _____

mf molto espr. *f* *rit*

a tempo *Ped.* *L.H.*

149

WHEN THE CHILDREN ARE ASLEEP

Lyrics by **OSCAR HAMMERSTEIN** II / Music by **RICHARD RODGERS**

CAROUSEL (1945)

When we've tucked the kids in their down-y beds, and list-ened to each one

pray, We'll kiss the tops of their tous-led heads and

tip-toe qui-et-ly a-way. We'll tip-toe in-to our

YOU'LL NEVER WALK ALONE

Lyrics by **OSCAR HAMMERSTEIN** II / Music by **RICHARD RODGERS**

CAROUSEL (1945)

20th Century-Fox presents

RODGERS AND HAMMERSTEIN'S NEW STATE FAIR

STARRING **PAT BOONE** **BOBBY DARIN** **PAMELA TIFFIN** **ANN-MARGRET** **TOM EWELL** AND **ALICE FAYE** as MELISSA

PRODUCED BY **CHARLES BRACKETT** DIRECTED BY **JOSE FERRER** SCREENPLAY BY **RICHARD BREEN**

ADAPTATION BY
OSCAR HAMMERSTEIN II / **SONYA LEVIEN** / **PAUL GREEN**

CINEMASCOPE
COLOR BY DE LUXE

MUSIC SUPERVISED & CONDUCTED BY
ALFRED NEWMAN

STATE FAIR, originally a movie in 1945, was remade in 1962, receiving the full Cinemascope treatment. Alice Faye returned to the movies for this version after a long absence.

JUNE IS BUSTIN' OUT ALL OVER

Lyrics by **OSCAR HAMMERSTEIN** II / Music by **RICHARD RODGERS**

CAROUSEL (1945)

wheels be - side a mill!_____ June is bust-in' out all
kit - ten - ish with pap!_____ June is bust-in' out all
grab her by the gills!_____ June is bust-in' out all

o - ver!_____ The feel - in' is get - tin' so in -
o - ver!_____ To la - dies the men are pay - in'
o - ver!_____ The sheep are - n't sleep - in' an - y

tense,_____ That the young Vir - gin - ia creep - ers Hev been
court._____ Lots - a ships are kept at an - chor Jest be -
more!_____ All the rams that chase the ewe sheep Are de -

IT MIGHT AS WELL BE SPRING

Lyrics by **OSCAR HAMMERSTEIN** II / Music by **RICHARD RODGERS**

STATE FAIR (1945)

The things I used to like I don't like an-y more, I want a lot of oth-er things I've nev-er had be-fore. It's just like moth-er says, I "sit a-round and mope" Pre-tend-ing I am won-der-ful and know-ing I'm a dope. ____

Above: Jeanne Crain and Dana Andrews in STATE FAIR (1945).

Right: Oscar Hammerstein II at work in the early 1940's.

Below:

The original sheet music title page for the film STATE FAIR.

Original sheet music title page from CENTENNIAL SUMMER from which comes the lovely Hammerstein-Kern standard "All Through The Day."

IT'S A GRAND NIGHT FOR SINGING

Lyrics by **OSCAR HAMMERSTEIN** II / Music by **RICHARD RODGERS**

STATE FAIR (1945)

It's a grand night for sing - ing! The moon is fly - ing high _____ And some-where a bird who is

173

ALL THROUGH THE DAY

Lyrics by **OSCAR HAMMERSTEIN II** / Music by **JEROME KERN**   **CENTENNIAL SUMMER** (1946)

YOU ARE NEVER AWAY

Lyrics by **OSCAR HAMMERSTEIN** II / Music by **RICHARD RODGERS**

ALLEGRO (1947)

Although not the success of its predecessors OKLAHOMA! and CAROUSEL, ALLEGRO gave Oscar Hammerstein the chance to essaye new and challenging directions for the musical theatre. Above: The full company. Below: Roberta Jonay and John Battles in ALLEGRO (1947).

ALLEGRO - original sheet music title page. Insert at lower right: Annamary Dickey, Lisa Kirk, John Battles, Roberta Jonay, William Ching (bottom row); John Conte, Muriel O'Malley, Paul Parks, Lily Paget (top row).

THE GENTLEMAN IS A DOPE

Lyrics by **OSCAR HAMMERSTEIN** II / Music by **RICHARD RODGERS**

ALLEGRO (1947)

up! The gen-tle-man gets me down!

The gen-tle-man is a dope — a man of man-y faults, — A

clum-sy Joe who would-n't know a Rhum-ba from a Waltz. The

gen-tle-man is a dope — and not my cup of tea. — (Why

187

do I get in a dith - er? He does - n't be - long ____ to

me!) ____ The gen - tle-man is - n't bright, ____ he

does - n't know the score ____ A cake will come, he'll take a crumb and

nev - er ask for more! The gen - tle-man's eyes are blue ____ but

SO FAR

Lyrics by **OSCAR HAMMERSTEIN** II / Music by **RICHARD RODGERS**

ALLEGRO (1947)

PIANO

No keep - sakes_ have we of days that_ are gone, . No

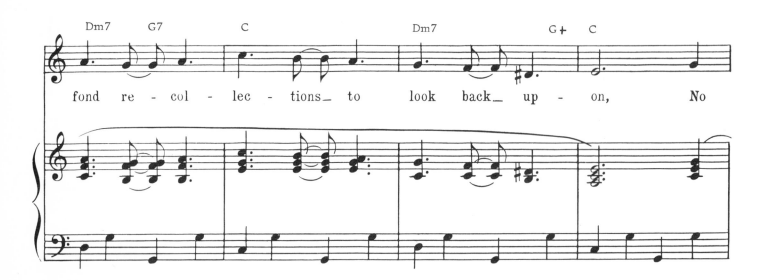

fond re - col - lec - tions_ to look back_ up - on, No

we have noth-ing to re-mem-ber so far, so far, But

now I'm face to face with you and now at last we've met, And

now we can look for-ward to the things we'll nev-er for-

1. get!

2. get!

HONEY BUN

Lyrics by **OSCAR HAMMERSTEIN** II / Music by **RICHARD RODGERS**

SOUTH PACIFIC (1949)

My doll is as dain - ty as a spar - row, ___ Her fig - ure is some - thing to ap - plaud. Where she's nar - row she's nar - row as an ar - row, ___ And she's broad, where a broad, should be broad. ___

A hun-dred and one pounds of fun,— That's my lit-tle Hon-ey-bun!—

Get a load of Hon-ey-bun to - night.———— I'm

speak-in' of my Sweet-ie Pie,— On-ly six-ty inch-es high,—

Ev-'ry inch is packed with dy - na - mite! ———— Her

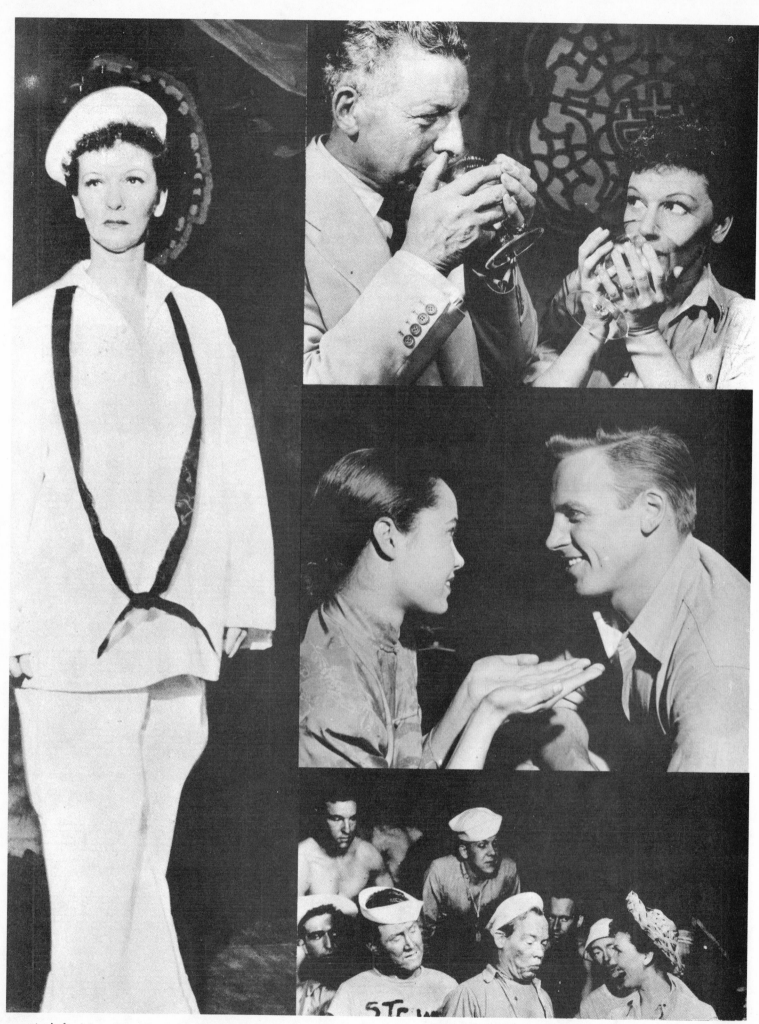

At left: Mary Martin as Nellie Forbush in SOUTH PACIFIC. Top: Ezio Pinza and Mary Martin. Center: Betta St. John and William Tabbert sing "Happy Talk" and at the bottom Mary Martin with Henry Slate and Myron McCormick (foreground).

THIS NEARLY WAS MINE

Lyrics by **OSCAR HAMMERSTEIN** II / Music by **RICHARD RODGERS**

SOUTH PACIFIC (1949)

A COCK-EYED OPTIMIST

Lyrics by **OSCAR HAMMERSTEIN** II / Music by **RICHARD RODGERS**

SOUTH PACIFIC (1949)

HAPPY TALK

Lyrics by **OSCAR HAMMERSTEIN** II / Music by **RICHARD RODGERS**

SOUTH PACIFIC (1949)

Top: Ezio Pinza, Barbara Luna, Michael DeLeon, and Mary Martin. Left: Juanita Hall sings "Happy Talk". Center: The writers, director and producer Leland Hayward at Mary Martin's last performance in SOUTH PACIFIC, 1951. Bottom: Miss Martin presents a Medal to Hammerstein at Dutch Treat Club Dinner, April 10, 1958.

Above: Mary Martin sings of her "Wonderful Guy." Below: "The March of the Siamese Children" in the film version of THE KING AND I with Deborah Kerr and Yul Brynner.

YOUNGER THAN SPRINGTIME

Lyrics by **OSCAR HAMMERSTEIN** II / Music by **RICHARD RODGERS**

SOUTH PACIFIC (1949)

GETTING TO KNOW YOU

Lyrics by **OSCAR HAMMERSTEIN** II / Music by **RICHARD RODGERS**

It's a ver - y an - cient say - ing But a true and hon - est thought, That if you be - come a teach - er, by your pu - pils you'll be taught. As a teach - er, I've been

learn‑ing (You'll for‑give me if I boast.) And I've now be‑come an

ex‑pert On the sub‑ject I like most, Get‑ting to know you.

REFRAIN (gracefully, not fast)

Get‑ting to know you, get‑ting to know all a‑bout you ___

___ Get‑ting to like you, get‑ting to hope you like me ___

SHALL WE DANCE?

Lyrics by **OSCAR HAMMERSTEIN** II / Music by **RICHARD RODGERS**

THE KING AND I (1951)

We've just been in-tro-duced, I do not know you well. But when the mu-sic start-ed, some-thing drew me to your side. So

man - y men and girls Are in each oth - er's arms, It

made me think we might be sim - i - lar - ly oc - cu - pied.

REFRAIN (Gai ly)

Shall we dance?

On a bright cloud of

mu - sic shall we fly?

Shall we dance?

oth - er, And shall you be my new ro - mance? _____

_ On the clear un - der - stand - ing that this

kind of thing can hap - pen, Shall we dance? Shall we dance? Shall we

1. dance?

2. Shall we dance? _____

Above: Richard Rodgers and Oscar Hammerstein II at work writing THE KING AND I, one of their legendary shows and a classic of the modern musical theatre (1951).

Below: The original sheet music title pages for the Hollywood and Broadway versions of THE KING AND I. In the center is the Playbill cover with Gertrude Lawrence who created the role of schoolteacher Anna Leonowens on the Broadway stage.

Yul Brynner became a "star" with his portrayal of the King of Siam in THE KING AND I. Brynner re-created his role for the 20th Century Fox film of THE KING AND I giving a magnetic and moving performance.

I WHISTLE A HAPPY TUNE

Lyrics by **OSCAR HAMMERSTEIN** II / Music by **RICHARD RODGERS**

THE KING AND I (1951)

shoes I strike a care-less pose And whis-tle a hap-py tune And no-one ev-er knows I'm a-fraid The re-sult of this de-cep-tion is ver-y strange to tell For when I fool the peo-ple I fear, I

fool my-self as well! I whis-tle a hap-py tune And

ev-'ry sin-gle time The hap-pi-ness in the tune con-

vin-ces me that I'm not a - fraid.

Coda

Make be-lieve you're brave And the trick will take you far.

HELLO, YOUNG LOVERS

Lyrics by **OSCAR HAMMERSTEIN** II / Music by **RICHARD RODGERS**

THE KING AND I (1951)

star, Be brave and faith-ful and true _____

Cling ver-y close to each oth-er to-night ___ I've been in

love like you. _____ I know how it feels to have

wings on your heels, And to fly down a street in a trance. ___

MY LORD AND MY MASTER

Lyrics by **OSCAR HAMMERSTEIN** II / Music by **RICHARD RODGERS**

THE KING AND I (1951)

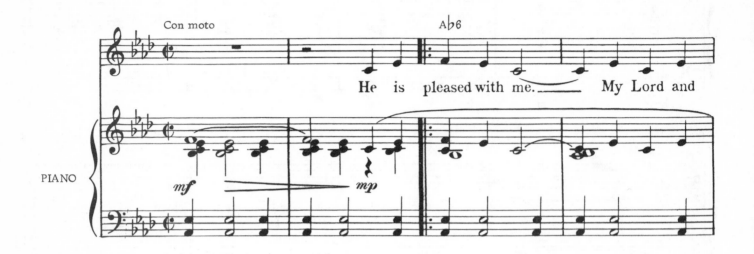

He is pleased with me.____ My Lord and

Mas - ter ____ De - clares he's pleased with me, ____ what does he

mean? ____ What does he know of me, ____ this Lord and

Mas - ter?_____ When he has looked at me, _____ what has he

seen?_____ Some - thing young, soft and slim,

Paint - ed cheek, tap -'ring limb, Smil - ing lips all for him.

Eyes that shine just for him, So he thinks _____ just for

Bill Hayes and Isabel Bigley in ME AND JULIET (1953).

Original sheet music title page for ME AND JULIET. Below: Helen Traubel and William Johnson in PIPE DREAM (1955).

Above: Judy Tyler and Helen Traubel in PIPE DREAM. Below: Playbill cover and original sheet music title page for PIPE DREAM.

I'M YOUR GIRL

Lyrics by **OSCAR HAMMERSTEIN II** / Music by **RICHARD RODGERS**

ME AND JULIET (1953)

Once and for al-ways let me make it clear, What I am to you and what you are to me. I want to tell you while I have you near, This is how it is and how it's going to be.

REFRAIN
(Slowly, with warm expression)

I'm your girl, it's time you knew, All I
am be-longs to you. An - y time you're
out of luck ___ I'm un-luck-y too. ___
I'm your part-ner, your lov-er, your wife, your

248

A VERY SPECIAL DAY

Lyrics by **OSCAR HAMMERSTEIN** II / Music by **RICHARD RODGERS**

ME AND JULIET (1953)

THE BIG BLACK GIANT

Lyrics by **OSCAR HAMMERSTEIN** II / Music by **RICHARD RODGERS**

ME AND JULIET (1953)

The wa-ter in a riv-er is changed ev-'ry day as it flows from the hills to the

sea, But to peo-ple on the shore, the riv-er is the same, or at

least, it ap-pears to be. The aud-ience in a thea-tre is

laugh-ing gi - ant; An-oth-er night a weep-ing gi - ant.

One night it's a cough-ing gi - ant; An-oth-er night a

sleep-ing gi - ant. Ev-'ry night you fight the gi-ant and

may-be if you win, You send him out a

nic - er gi - ant than he was when he came in... But

poco rit.

if he does-n't like you, then all you can do is to pack up your make-up and

go. For an act-or in a flop, there is - n't an-y choice, but to look for an-oth - er

show._____ That big black gi-ant who

Above: Rodgers and Hammerstein. Below: Oscar Hammerstein II during a FLOWER DRUM SONG rehearsal in 1958.

Above: Lesley Ann Warren and Stuart Damon in CINDERELLA with Pat Carroll, Barbara Ruick, and Celeste Holm (2nd row), Jo Van Fleet, Ginger Rogers and Walter Pigeon (top row). Below: Pat Carroll, Barbara Ruick, and Jo Van Fleet.

EVERYBODY'S GOT A HOME BUT ME

Lyrics by **OSCAR HAMMERSTEIN II** / Music by **RICHARD RODGERS**

PIPE DREAM (1955)

THE NEXT TIME IT HAPPENS

Lyrics by **OSCAR HAMMERSTEIN** II / Music by **RICHARD RODGERS**

PIPE DREAM (1955)

Allegretto

PIANO

I leapt be-fore I looked And I got hooked. I played with fire and burned, That's how I learned. I must ad-mit I owe a lot to you. From now on I will know what not to do.

THE MAN I USED TO BE

Lyrics by **OSCAR HAMMERSTEIN** II / Music by **RICHARD RODGERS**

PIPE DREAM (1955)

TEN MINUTES AGO

Lyrics by **OSCAR HAMMERSTEIN** II / Music by **RICHARD RODGERS**

CINDERELLA (1957)

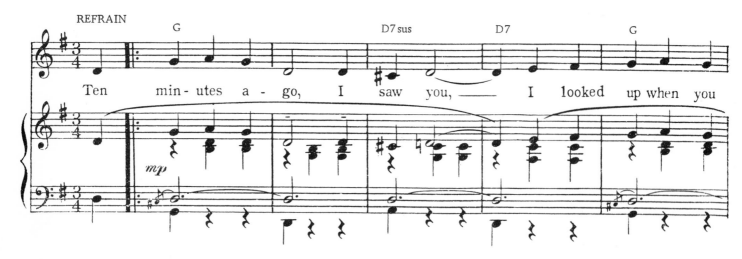

Left: Juanita hall, Miyoshi Umeki, Keye Luke in FLOWER DRUM SONG. Above and below: Original sheet music title pages and Playbill cover.

Below left: Pat Suzuki and dancers enliven FLOWER DRUM SONG with a sultry dance number. Center: Keye Luke. Right: Sheet music title page for the film version.

A LOVELY NIGHT

Lyrics by **OSCAR HAMMERSTEIN** II / Music by **RICHARD RODGERS**

CINDERELLA (1957)

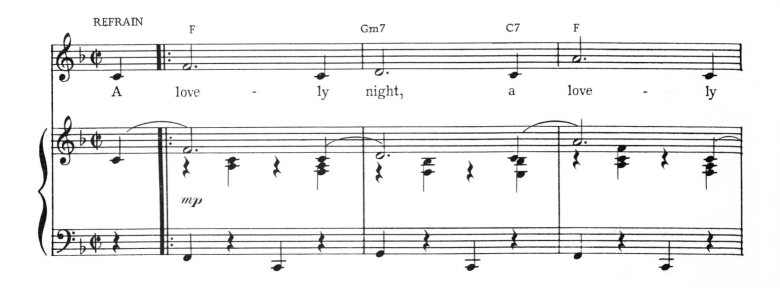

IN MY OWN LITTLE CORNER

Lyrics by **OSCAR HAMMERSTEIN** II / Music by **RICHARD RODGERS**

CINDERELLA (1957)

game I can play with a cool and con-fi-dent kind of

air,_____ Just as long as I stay in my own lit-tle

cor - ner,_____ All a - lone in my own lit-tle

1.

chair. In my

2.

chair._____

YOU ARE BEAUTIFUL

Lyrics by **OSCAR HAMMERSTEIN II** / Music by **RICHARD RODGERS**   **FLOWER DRUM SONG** (1958)

Above: THE SOUND OF MUSIC with Mary Martin (left) and Julie Andrews in the film version (right). Below: Mary Martin with the Von Trapp children in the Broadway production.

MY BEST LOVE

Lyrics by **OSCAR HAMMERSTEIN** II / Music by **RICHARD RODGERS**

FLOWER DRUM SONG (1958)

How can a young man know where his heart will go?

On-ly an old man knows what a man should know.

All that was true for

SUNDAY

Lyrics by **OSCAR HAMMERSTEIN** II / Music by **RICHARD RODGERS**

FLOWER DRUM SONG (1958)

DON'T MARRY ME

Lyrics by **OSCAR HAMMERSTEIN** II / Music by **RICHARD RODGERS**

FLOWER DRUM SONG (1958)

(Sammy) You are young and beau-ti-ful,___ Sweet as the breath of May.___ Ear-nest-ly I speak to you.___ Weigh ev-'ry word I say.

CLIMB EV'RY MOUNTAIN

Lyrics by **OSCAR HAMMERSTEIN** II / Music by **RICHARD RODGERS**

THE SOUND OF MUSIC (1959)

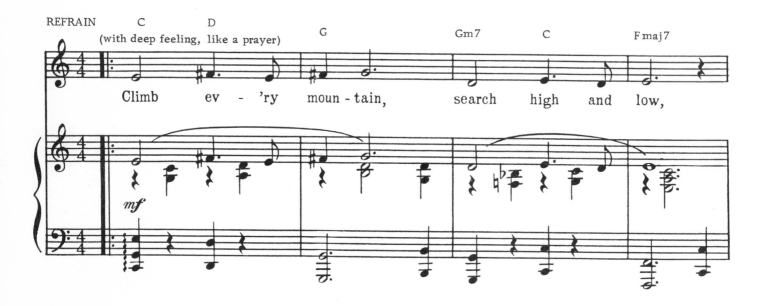

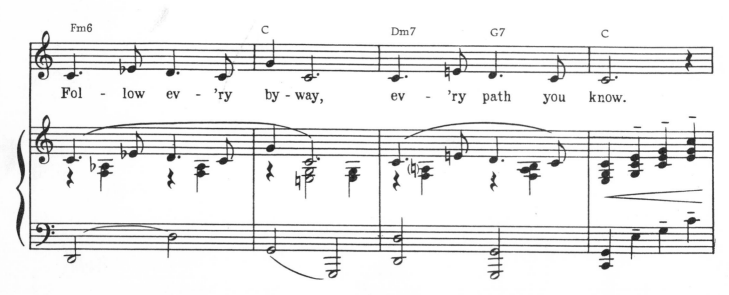

Above: Julie Andrews and the Von Trapp children in the spectacular film version of THE SOUND OF MUSIC. It seems fitting that Oscar Hammerstein's last show became one of the most successful and top-grossing films of all time. Below left: The Von Trapps sing "Edelweiss" in a dramatic scene from the film. Center: Playbill cover for the Broadway show. Right: Sheet music title page for THE LAST TIME I SAW PARIS which featured the Hammerstein-Kern song of the same name.

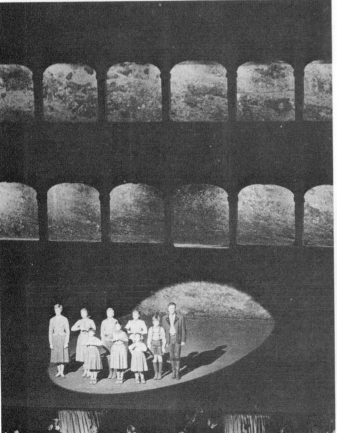

MY FAVORITE THINGS

Lyrics by **OSCAR HAMMERSTEIN II** / Music by **RICHARD RODGERS**

THE SOUND OF MUSIC (1959)

When I'm feel-ing sad, _____ I sim-ply re-mem-ber my fa-vor-ite things and then I don't feel so bad. _____

EDELWEISS

Lyrics by **OSCAR HAMMERSTEIN** II / Music by **RICHARD RODGERS**

THE SOUND OF MUSIC (1959)

312

THE LAST TIME I SAW PARIS

Lyrics by **OSCAR HAMMERSTEIN** II / Music by **JEROME KERN** Interpolated into the films **LADY, BE GOOD** (1941) and **THE LAST TIME I SAW PARIS** (1954)

SHOW
CHRONOLOGY
AND INDEX OF SONGS

SHOW/SONG/PAGE	Theatre	Opening	No. of Performances
ROSE-MARIE Indian Love Call, 16 Rose-Marie, 12	Imperial	9/2/24	557
SUNNY Who?, 20	New Amsterdam	9/22/25	517
THE DESERT SONG The Desert Song, 33 One Alone, 29 The Riff Song, 24	Casino	11/30/26	465
SHOW BOAT Can't Help Lovin' Dat Man, 36 Make Believe, 42 Ol' Man River, 57 Why Do I Love You?, 52 You Are Love, 46	Ziegfeld	12/26/27	575
THE NEW MOON Lover, Come Back To Me, 66 Stouthearted Men, 62 Wanting You, 70	Imperial	9/19/28	519
SWEET ADELINE Don't Ever Leave Me, 75 Why Was I Born?, 78	Hammerstein	9/3/29	233
MUSIC IN THE AIR I've Told Ev'ry Little Star, 82 The Song Is You, 86	Alvin	11/8/32	146
HIGH, WIDE AND HANDSOME (Film) A Paramount Pictures Release The Folks Who Live On The Hill, 91	-----	7/22/37	-----
VERY WARM FOR MAY All In Fun, 100 All The Things You Are, 96 In The Heart Of The Dark, 106	Alvin	11/17/39	59
OKLAHOMA! I Cain't Say No, 114 Many A New Day, 120 Oh, What A Beautiful Mornin', 124 Oklahoma, 110 Pore Jud, 128	St. James	3/31/43	2,212
CARMEN JONES Beat Out Dat Rhythm On A Drum, 140 Dat's Love, 134	Broadway	12/2/43	502

SHOW/SONG/PAGE	Theatre	Opening	No. of Performances
CAROUSEL If I Loved You, 146 June Is Bustin' Out All Over, 158 When The Children Are Asleep, 150 You'll Never Walk Alone, 154	Majestic	4/19/45	800
STATE FAIR (Film) A 20th Century Fox Release It Might As Well Be Spring, 164 It's A Grand Night For Singing, 170	-----	8/20/45	-----
CENTENNIAL SUMMER (Film) A 20th Century Fox Release All Through The Day, 174	-----	5/29/46	-----
ALLEGRO The Gentleman Is A Dope, 186 So Far, 192 You Are Never Away, 178	Majestic	10/10/47	315
SOUTH PACIFIC A Cock-Eyed Optimist, 206 Happy Talk, 210 Honey Bun, 196 This Nearly Was Mine, 201 Younger Than Springtime, 218	Majestic	4/7/49	1,925
THE KING AND I Getting To Know You, 222 Hello, Young Lovers, 236 I Whistle A Happy Tune, 232 My Lord And Master, 242 Shall We Dance?, 226	St. James	3/29/51	1,246
ME AND JULIET The Big Black Giant, 254 I'm Your Girl, 247 A Very Special Day, 250	Majestic	5/28/53	358
PIPE DREAM Everybody's Got A Home But Me, 262 The Man I Used To Be, 270 The Next Time It Happens, 266	Shubert	11/30/55	246
CINDERELLA (Television) A CBS-TV Production In My Own Little Corner, 282 A Lovely Night, 279 Ten Minutes Ago, 274	-----	3/3/57	-----
FLOWER DRUM SONG Don't Marry Me, 298 My Best Love, 290 Sunday, 294 You Are Beautiful, 286	St. James	12/1/58	600
THE SOUND OF MUSIC Climb Ev'ry Mountian, 304 Edelweiss, 312 My Favorite Things, 308	Lunt-Fontanne	11/16/59	1,443
MISCELLANEOUS The Last Time I Saw Paris, 315 Used in Lady Be Good - Film (1941) and in The Last Time I Saw Paris - Film (1954)	-----	-----	-----